Knowing Your Child

Mario Cesar
Knowing Your Child

All inquiries should be addressed to: Mario Cesar Mariocesar2711@gmail.com

—

Published by - Spines
ISBN: 979-8-89569-541-8

Knowing Your Child

Discover your child's personality through their astrological signs

Mario Cesar

I dedicate this book to a Cancer sign who has inspired me and given me that bit of pleasure, inner satisfaction, love, and energy that without him I could not have written this Astrology book for parents to know their children.

To my son, Alexis Bernard, and also my granddaughters Zoey Michelle, Nora Juliette, and Lydia Violette who has been able to give new meaning to my life, and has become my safest source of inspiration.

Memo from a Child to the Parents

Don't spoil me. I know very well that I cannot have everything I want (actually, the only thing I want to put you to the test).

Do not be afraid to be severe with me: this is how I will make you feel more secure.

Don't let me form bad habits, well I depend entirely on you to know what is good or bad.

Don't make me feel smaller than I am. That would only lead me to act as if I were a big spoiled.

Do not correct me or yell at me in front of other people. If you speak to me in private, and without shouting, I will understand you better.

Don't magnify the consequences of my mistakes, sometimes I need to learn in a painful and realistic way.

Do not try to protect me: you would be doing me more harm than good.

Don't get mad when I tell you I hate you. It's not you guys I hate, it's your ability to make me feel frustrated.

Don't take my little complaints or discomforts too serious. On many occasions I am just a way to attract your attention.

Don't waste time pestering me or scolding me: I will always protect myself by playing deaf.

Don't forget that I can't express myself the way you do. That's why you think I'm not always right.

Don't discourage me with your silence when I ask you questions. If you don't help me, I'll go find the answers I need elsewhere.

Don't contradict each other in front of me. That can confuse me and make me lose faith in you.

Don't tell me my fears or fears are silly. They are terrifyingly real to me, and you can do a lot to give me the reassurance I need.

Don't make me believe that you are perfect and infallible. The surprise that would take me to discover that you are not could be traumatic.

Never think that you are humiliating yourself when you have to apologize to me. An honest apology would increase my respect and affection for you.

Don't forget that I love to experiment; it's something I can't live or grow without.

Please try to understand and support me.
Always try to be by my side during my growth. I know it's hard but please don't stop trying.

Never forget that without love and understanding I can neither grow nor exist: Please stay physically and mentally healthy: I need you.

Introduction

This book is a guide for parents, grandparents, uncles, teachers, babysitters and all those who love and want to know the personality, emotions, feelings, individuality and behavior of that loved one who is a child. In its pages, you will find the astral influences that gravitate over that child so close to your heart. To achieve this, I have relied on an ancient science, Astrology, whose main discovery has been finding a relationship between human character and personality and the stars of our galaxy.

What is Astrology?

Astrology can be defined as the recovery of consciousness or the discovery on the part of us, the terrestrial ones, of the complex interrelation that we have with the stars of this galaxy.

It has not been an easy discovery. To get to what we know today as Astrology, a process of centuries has been required, in which hundreds of generations of wise men and scholars have invested the best of their lives. For this reason, the sophisticated material that reaches your hands today (in the form of daily horoscopes and Home Maps) is not the admirable result of those of the sudden ideas of some great individuals, but the realization of a collective work of centuries, to through which man has been able to start the long and fruitful path of reconciliation with the Universe.

However, the link between the intuitive mind and the rational mind that has been so brilliantly achieved by Astrology has had to face, over the centuries, the resistance of the intellectual and the ignorant at the same time. The former, trusting in the powers of their intellect, tend to forget about the influence of the spirit on their actions and thoughts, and therefore deny the importance of Astrology and its contributions to the knowledge of human destiny. The latter, fearful that something will be revealed to them that does not agree with the image they have made of their own micro-universe, also refuse to accept the discoveries of this ancient discipline.

But this resistance has not succeeded in stopping the advance of Astrology, nor has it prevented it from demonstrating how useful it can be in helping human beings in the contemplation of themselves and their relationships with those around them.

We must not forget, however, that there are other relationships (socio-economic, cultural, geographical, and sexual) that do not fit within the astro-human relationship. In the case of children, for example, the sex of the child must be taken into account, if he is an only child and his place within the group of siblings with whom he must live (if he is the first-born, the youngest or the second), when the time comes to explain his character and behavior.

You may wonder: What, then, is the usefulness of Astrology in the task of understanding and guiding the character of our children?

The answer is simple: Astrology is irreplaceable in the task of explaining why two children from the same socio-economic level and from the same cultural and biological circumstances can have such different personalities.

The Personality of Children at Birth.

From the moment a child arrives in this world, they are already showing their own personality. You wonder, why? When I asked myself the same question, the idea of writing this book was born. As I am not a psychologist, nor do I intend to become one, my fundamental guide to arrive at an answer to such a difficult question was Astrology.

The reason is not so difficult to explain: If children arrive in this world without the expressive resources that adults have (the word above all), our task should be to try to find a way to know the reactions, the feelings and the child's mental processes when he cannot yet express himself in the way we do.

Astrology, which gives some general lines to describe the personality of your child according to the study of certain relationships between his date of birth and the situation of the stars in our galaxy, is perhaps one of the few disciplines that could help us in this complex, but fun task.

If you assume, as I do, that our children think and feel for themselves and that certain fundamental traits of their personality can be explained through the logical procedures of Astrology, this book can be useful in the difficult process of understanding and guide the character of your children in the first years of their life.

Aided by the model offered by Astrology, you would be able to stimulate the positive tendencies of your baby's character and correct, as far as possible, the defects that could affect them. (I must clarify that the recommendations offered by Astrology are not unrelated to the studies that have been carried out on the behavior of babies in recent years. On the contrary, there is a close relationship between the discoveries of researchers in this field and astrological perception.

I am sure that at this point in my story, you will have discovered that choosing this age (between birth and two years) for this book is not by chance. It is at that decisive age that our children are most dependent on us, not only in the strict physical and biological sense, but also emotionally. In no other period of their lives will their world revolve in such a decisive way around our actions, nor will they be willing to offer us their affection and unlimited love, nor will the changes observed in their behavior be so great and decisive. This book is only intended to be a guide for those two years in which you and your baby will live the most exciting period of your lives.

Contents

Aries

From March 21 to April 20

"I AM"

It symbolizes birth. The beginning and awakening to a new stage. It is the first step of the pioneer, making his own way, despite the odds. Difficulties, to get an important place in life. It is the being itself; the child's ego in search of its own affirmation.

How Aries Thinks

How, are you paying attention to me? Are you sure you are listening only to me? it is better that you are doing it because I am from Aries, the first sign of the Zodiac, the most warrior of the signs, the only one that is symbolized by a huge "I Am" (bigger than my crib and the car in the that you walk me sometimes). It's not that I'm conceited or that I pretend the world begins and ends with me. What happens is that my sign is ruled by the planet Mars (Do you remember Mars? The God of war, the one who accompanied Achilles on his craziest expeditions) and I belong the same than the signs Leo and Sagittarius to the element Fire (the one that gives heat and makes the heart beat). Due to the meeting of these two very vibrant and active friends, I am a restless child, full of energy and dynamism, tireless in my games, always willing to learn something new.

My powerful dynamism has its roots in a very ancient history. It is said that Phrixus the son of Athama and Nepheles, was to be sacrificed in honor of to the gods for Ino, his evil stepmother. Hermes (Mercury) to help the boy in danger sent him a ram whose most visible characteristic possessed a golden fleece. Phrixus and his sister Helles escaped by flying through the air on the ram's back.

Along the way, Helles fell and drowned in a river that today bears his name, the Hellespont. Phrixus arrived at his destination, sacrificed the ram and hung the Golden Fleece from the grove of Ares or Mars. There that the sign of the golden ram (Aries) means the ability to overcome the most difficult obstacles. If you see me wanting to leave my crib, I love to give you several tips: First, do not panic. As the good adventurer that I am, from my first days I want to become a daring explorer, not recoil from any danger and enjoy the greatest risks. Second, don't try to stop it. If you do, you must not only suffer one of my tantrums, if not later you will have to regret having suppressed my adventurous instincts. Third, instead of playing the boring and tiring role of the fearful parents, become my accomplices and participate in my adventure. You will see how fun the world of Aries children is.

Hmm! It seems that I already hinted at the keyword "Understanding" if there is the key to how to treat me, the Aries boy or girl. If you are understanding with me and do not try to force me to follow your wishes, there will not be a child bolder, happier, more creative and more loving than me. But if you decide on the ogre's strategy and make my life miserable with your scolding, your orders and your cries of incomprehension, you will have to deal with a capricious, stubborn, willful, aggressive and selfish little rebel! Oh! I was forgetting a fourth possibility: if you opt for the boredom line and left alone with nothing to do, I'll turn into a short- tempered child, ready to unleash all my wasted energy on him first object, person or animal that crosses my path.

My adventuring partners, the Aries girls, are very much like me: active, independent, full of energy, always ready to be the first to travel through unknown territories. Try to treat them with the same methods that work for other zodiac signs and you will find unpleasant surprises: instead of the obedient and docile girl who follows her parents' orders to the letter, you will have to deal with a small rebellious who does not accept any obstacle to her vitality and initiative. This does not mean, however, that you should have no role in our education. On the contrary, it depends, to a large extend, on you how happy we can become in our lives.

Except that with us, the Arians, everything depends on the style and tact with which we are treated. A smile, a look full of love, a word of encouragement, are worth much more to us than a thousand warnings and prohibitions. (That's right: don't forget to pay attention to me when I launch into conquer the world. So much vitality increases the dangers of having an accident). Especially on the face and head. If you meet an Aries child with a contemplative and calm temperament, don't think that everything said here has no validity. It is simply that this child has some of the characteristics of the opposite sign, Libra (the sign of union and harmony or possibly another sign in the ascendant).

From Birth to One Year Aries

Even before being born, I, the Aries child, will make my presence known to you with my tireless kicking and my continuous movement of my arms. And when, finally, I arrive in this world, no one can say that you could not find out about my arrival: the noise I make is so great that even the most reticent have to acknowledge my triumphant arrival.

As if from a very young age I knew what I wanted, my parents will have to get used to my vigorous movements, an early sign of impatience coming from the obvious imbalance between the pace that I would like to impose on my development and the one that reality and you owe me. Suggest, and learn to interpret them as a way to express my discontent with the state of things around me.

But not even your suggestions, nor the obvious limits imposed by human biology, will prevent me from taking my first steps in this world at seven months, which I suppose is made to be conquered by me in the shortest possible time. Therefore, don't be surprised to see me trying to move forward clinging to the nearest furniture, and don't look surprised, when instead of falling asleep, as our peers from other signs would do, we jump around in our crib with unusual energy.

In nine months, you will see me fighting against the

law of gravity, falling to the ground from time to time, and getting up again, with renewed energy, ready to leave the narrow framework of my room and, a little later, the very narrow framework of my house. When I finally manage to take a few steps without ending up on the ground, your sincere applause will fill me with happiness and pride, and I will feel that all the effort I have made has been worth it.

From One to Two Years Aries

Our well-earned prestige as individualists and independents will make itself felt when we start walking. So, we will want to do everything on our own and try to excel every chance we get. You will watch with increasing pride as your little Aries child is the one who decides what should be played, where and with what rules. Over time, however, you will realize that our independence does not end with playing with our little friends, but extends to our relationships with you. Therefore, do not be surprised if you see us insist, with devastating force, on something that we want, or if we do not want to follow the suggestions that you have proposed to us.

That is our character and only your ability to win our hearts can help us in the very difficult task of becoming obedient and reasonable children. When we reach eighteen months, it is recommended that all objects that may imply physical danger be removed from our reach. This does not mean, however, that all our vital energy should be wasted; On the contrary, your salvation as parents lies in you being able to design and promote the games that involve the greatest amount of action and the greatest possible expenditure of our endless energies. Push and pull toys, balls of all sizes and styles, rocking horses and toy hammers can be some of the toys that could help give our overflowing vitality an outlet.

If you want to know more about me, it would be recommendable that you get to know my Natal Map and find out what the sign of my Ascendant is and where the other planets are located. Then, you could get even closer to my true being, and understand how valuable it is for me to enjoy the independence and freedom that allow me to be as "I Am".

Taurus

From April 21 to May 20

"I HAVE"

It symbolizes the need to have a secure base. That is to say, possessing, retaining and preserving what Aries achieved and that Taurus accumulated with more perseverance. His instinct is based on an interest in acquiring personal values and resources. The child of this sign will always seek his own stability.

How Taurus Thinks

I guess you've already heard some of the things that are said about me being a boring and stubborn, conservative and ambitious child, obsessed with treasuring all the things that come my way. I do not deny that I have a point. But it is only part of the story. That we like to own and have, there is no doubt: for some reason the key phrase that defines me is "I have". However, that is not all, since my element is Earth (like my friends from the signs Virgo and Capricorn) I am endowed with a stability that would be the envy of any of the parents of children born under the influence of the Fire element as is the case with my Aries neighbors.

But what those who talk about my possible defects do not forget that I am ruled by Venus, the planet of beauty and love, the one that produces permanent and lasting feelings, the one that makes the finest gourmets and the most imaginative gardeners just like my Libra friends. That is why it is not surprising that you see me smile at the sound of some melody that my ears begin to enjoy or surprise me trying to use a pencil or brush, with the obvious intention of capturing my artistic ideas in the nearest object. The best thing you can do at times like this is to encourage me in my creative adventures, be patient with the possible transformations that some of the furniture in the house may undergo, and send me to receive music, painting, or drawing lessons as soon as possible.

Perhaps all this can be understood better if I tell you a mythological story: Jupiter, the god of all gods, fell madly in love with beautiful Europe. Ready to conquer your love, -Jupiter disguised himself as a white bull and managed to become the maiden's much loved playmate. One day, with Europa on his back, the bull entered the waters of the sea and swam to the island of Crete, where a love crystallized, in whose memory Jupiter placed the bull in the heavens and gave life to the Taurus constellation.

Without trying to appear like a threatening and spoiled child, I give you another piece of advice: do not try to impose your will on me by force, because you will have to face my bad side: that of the capricious child who does not easily allow the will of others to be imposed on me. Then I will be boring and resentful, a real burden to anyone around me.

Since I love to hoard and possess, you will see me collect objects and people: everything that I consider mine should remain by my side or in its place. Of course: guided by my good taste, only I will try to treasure beautiful and harmonious things. The other thing, what does not fit within my Venusian mentality, will not even be considered.

Sometimes you will see me quiet and distant, as if I were tired of the world and its inhabitants. No, it's not that he's sick. The thing is that my fixed personality makes me very unsociable in my early years. Over time, however, that may wear off and then you will rarely see me alone.

My fellow Taurus girls share with me most of the characteristics that you are learning about. With a surprise: they are more active in games than girls of the same age from other signs and they always look healthy and strong, ready to undertake any activity in which their talent for order and harmony can be used.

I have a secret clue that I was leaving for last: if my characteristics are those of my opposite sign, Scorpio, I will be mysterious, intuitive and cunning, capable of grasping the intentions and weaknesses of others. (Something that would not happen if I responded to the normal characteristics of my sign). In that case, I would have the sensitivity and emotionality that I almost always lack.

Two final pieces of advice: take good care of my throat, my neck and my nose, as I am predisposed to suffer from tonsils, nasal passages and pharynx. And, above all, don't let me eat everything I want, because I have a tempting tendency towards gluttony and gluttony and I could end up being one of those fat kids that everyone laughs at. (What's more: on certain occasions, when I feel depressed, and when things don't go the way I want, I dedicate myself to eating to forget what is happening to me. Therefore, don't be fooled by my overly good eating: it can be a sign that something bad is happening to me.

From Birth to One Year Taurus

Mom herself can attest to it: there is no baby more peaceful and calmer than those born under our sign. When we arrive to this world, we do so in silence, as if we were still questioning our arrival on Earth and did not want to be awakened from the peaceful sleep in which we had been sheltered until the moment of birth. For this reason, our first months pass in total peace (something that cannot be said of the first days of my companions, of other signs).

This does not mean, however, that nothing outside of sleeping and dreaming happens to us in our first months. To be fair, we must recognize that, from time to time, we also feel hungry, lonely and long for the attention we deserve. The difference lies in the way in which we express our discontent: instead of throwing the tantrum that my little Aries friend would use in these cases, I would settle for some almost inaudible moans and a very low-decibel whine (as if, in truth, would not like to be heard, or would not want to disturb others). And if you show up on time and give me a gesture of affection or give me my favorite toy, I will go back to being the same silent and modest child that I have always been.

As for meals, I don't think there is a baby with fewer problems in this regard than me: faithful to the schedules that you set for me, broad in my tastes, always willing to devour everything that is offered, I am every mother's dream.

However, there is something I must decide (although give a little bit of the party we've been to so far): when they undertake the very customary, and sometimes dangerous, task of comparing my development with that of the neighboring children, you will suffer a little disappointment; your baby, so peaceful and obedient, does not seem to have reached the level of development that my peers from other signs have acquired without much effort. With sadness and concern, you will see how, when the neighbors' children are already taking their first steps, moving (with a certain musicality) the maracas and wanting to launch themselves into the outside world, I continue looking, with absolute attention, at the objects that hang of my crib, as if I were determined to discover the secret keys to its operation. What's more: when others are already running over the world, it is possible that I remain seated, observing everything from my privileged position, delighting in the objects that surround me, imagining new formations and designs, turning my toys into objects of experimentation.

From One to Two Years Taurus

When I start walking, it is very likely that my security blanket (remembers Lino, Carlitos' friend, Snoopy's companions) will never leave me, and that we will both face the dangers and adventures of the outside world. My natural tenderness will not only be expressed in my relationship with you: the objects that surround me, the toys that have always accompanied me (but also the new ones), and my little friends, will be able to enjoy my tenderness and affection.

If you want to see me happy, take me for a walk fresh air. Every time you propose it to me I will be more than ready. But don't try to force me to use my legs too much or walk for long distances. Understand that my learning pace is slower than that of other children and that trying to force me to do things outside my natural pace can be counterproductive.

Another good news: due to my extreme regularity and my sense of order, it is very likely that at 18 months he will already be asking to go to the bathroom. However, do not forget to supervise me when I do it, because my artistic spirit can lead me to convert what is produced into material for plastic expression.

If you want to know more about me, it would be

recommended that you know my Natal Map, what the sign of my Ascendant is, and where the other planets are located. Then, you would be even closer to my true personality.

Gemini

From May 22 to June 21

"I THINK"

It symbolizes language and communication. It is also necessary to specify things, ideas, and facts to establish bonds of friendship with children of other signs, through communication. It is the knowledge that seeks to develop intelligence. It is the concrete and analytical mind.

How Gemini Thinks

With me start the moment of complications. What like my Aries and Taurus friends could be reduced to a keyword (to be, to possess), in me becomes something more complicated and unpredictable: "I think." The apparent simplicity of these two words that contain all the mysteries of life humanity. Do not think, however, that it is some whim of our astrologer friends; It happens that, like my companions from Libra and Aquarius, I have the characteristics of the Air element, if you do not think about the story behind my sign: Leda, the fiancée of Tyndaro, king of Sparta, would have been visited by Jupiter, in the form of a beautiful swan. From the union of the two, twins, Castor and Pollux, would have been born. The first son of men and the second of the Gods. They were both educated by Mercury, the planet of communication and analysis, (which is our ruling planet like my Virgo companions) until it became the original model for all the Gemini children who have continued to come into this world, with our double nature, inherited from gods and men.

I am sure that at this point in my story, you will have already realized that duality predominates in me (don't be scared, it is not a disease). That is why you will always see me active, trying to decipher all the mysteries of the universe, to find the secret of all things, to find the most impossible relationships, to connect the most disparate objects and people. On the other hand, if you want to find in me the peaceful and calm child, who is captivated by seeing the same doll that you have left in front of my crib with that precise objective, you will suffer a terrible disappointment, because very soon I will have tired of the doll and I will be looking for new food for my insatiable curiosity.

I know that my extreme activity may surprise you and even irritate you at certain times. Don't think I don't understand you. What more could I expect from beings who have to witness my continuous movement, my attempts to turn everything around me into part of my games, my desire to make their tie or their new earrings pieces of my imaginary puzzle but I ask you, please, not to try to impose your points of view with the very weak argument of your parental authority, because then you are going to have a restless and nervous child, who can use cunning to get what he wants.

And although nobody likes to talk about their shortcomings, it seems that the time has come to talk about me: since I belong to the sign of duality, I can be one of those inventors without inventions, of those momentary geniuses, of those superficial beings who go from one thing to another without concentrating on any, then I will start a task or a game and abandon it after five minutes for a different one, that we are in the worst of sadness and can produce, in seconds, the most radiant of smiles. (By the way, another interesting fact: since I can do so many things at once, I love imitating people, repeating their gestures, rehearsing their faces and movements. Think, however, on the positive side of this trend, I could become an actor or a professional actor.

My sign and playmates, the Gemini girls, although they generally possess thc traits that I have already told you about, have some more things in their favor, due to their great communication skills and their continuous search for everything unknown. They can talk much faster than other children and become the center of attention wherever they are.

If by some design of fate, I was under the influence of the opposite sign, Sagittarius, I would be a happy, generous and independent child, capable of sharing with other children and of cheering up the most boring of situations with my joy.

Since I am such a restless and adventurous Child, my hands, arms and legs are at risk, as are my bronchial tubes and lungs, which can be seriously affected by a simple cold.

From Birth to One Year Gemini

From the very moment of our birth, Gemini babies are distinguished by our hypersensitivity and our continuous mood swings. The slightest noise can wake us up and when we are asleep we do not stop moving. Wanting to impose a schedule for meals and sleep is, most of the time, an illusion. Very soon, you will have to be at our side, trying to find out what is wrong with us. Gemini in the end, as always happens in these cases, you will have no alternative but to carry me in your arms, sing me a lullaby or propose some distraction that will get me out of boredom and the annoyance that your attempts to set schedules caused me.

But what can get me out of tiredness and boredom the fastest is for you to try to communicate with me. Don't laugh; this is a very serious recommendation. We Gemini children's love to communicate with others. In any way, but above all through words: if you tell us about an everyday event, or tell us about what is happening in the world, we will respond with babbling, hand movements and noises of all kinds. Very quickly you will realize that we have been trying to have a conversation very serious (with a few touches of humor, of course), and that if you don't get serious about the proposed exchange, your place in our hearts will be claiming that you do. When the conversation runs out, they can try the old method of giving us all kinds of toys to entertain us. The method - which has been used for generations in very diverse cultures-, has a small problem: very soon we will show our tiredness for the toys we have been given, and we will want to have new ones at our disposal. We all know, however, that the amount available can be easily depleted - especially if the child in question is a Gemini like us - and you would be left without any recourse to fight against our annoyance. But all is not lost: if by luck, you have toys that keep - and keep us- in constant movement, it is possible that the tantrum will pass and peace will return to your live.

From One to Two Years Gemini

Once we start walking, the crib and sleeping will lose all appeal for us. Not because we are restless and undisciplined children, who would enjoy disobeying the orders of our parents, but because by being able to walk, our world widens and our desire to know everything, to communicate with all the life that is outside the four walls of our house, multiplies and makes us think that dedicating precious time of exploration to sleep is nothing more than an immense waste of resources.

Luckily, in our exploratory enterprise we have the collaboration of very agile and strong legs, which are capable of taking us anywhere and also accompanying us in the inevitable falls that will come sooner or later. (One of our most desired goals is to get on the different tables that cross our path. We will do it again and again, without taking into account the falls, the failures, or the gifts from our loved ones.)

But not everything about us is pure physical action. You, our very lucky parents, will soon realize our unmatched ability to communicate and our passion for the spoken word. Thus, since we pass the act of being born, you will see us engaged in a fun, tireless struggle to acquire the language that allows us to communicate with you. At first, you will feel happy and proud to have a baby who, at such a young age, is already able to speak and handle a vocabulary that is considered out of reach. Later, however, they will feel a little annoyed, and even tired, by our tireless desire to talk. A good part of our character will depend on the way in which you face this situation: if you are patient and learn to enjoy your conversations with us and if you do not try to talk to us as if we did not understand anything, all the communicative capacity of babies of Gemini can be put into action; But if they are unsociable and uncomprehending, more concerned with their businesses and their world of big, boring people, it is possible that a good part of our potential will be lost and a certain resentment will grow in us.

Finally, one last, very useful piece of advice for our parents: if you want to see us peacefully asleep at the time you want, it is necessary that you follow the following instructions to the letter: sitting in a rocking chair, read us two entertaining illustrated books (we accept adventures from air, land, sea and space), and then sing us a beautiful lullaby (it doesn't matter if they go out of tune all the time: we will know how to forgive them for their mistakes). If after having followed this entire procedure to the letter, you are faced with the harsh reality of seeing us singing with you, without a hint of sleep and with energy to spare for several illustrated books and a few more songs, the best thing you can do It is to resign yourself and take advantage of the situation: What if these evenings allow you to discover the singer that was hidden in you or the storyteller that you never suspected existed within your soul.

If you want to reach my individual world, it would be important for you to know my Natal Map, where I have the Moon, what the sign of my Ascendant is and the location of the other planets. Then, you could get a little closer to my creative and complex world, and better understand my need to communicate with others.

Cancer

From June 22 to July 23

"I FEEL"

It symbolizes emotions, feelings and perceptions. It also represents home, family and country. He is protective of himself and other signs, appearing jealous, possessive and absorbing. It is the sign of intuition and psychic awakening. For this child, feelings come before everything.

How Cancer Thinks

So that I am not confused with the children of other signs of the Zodiac, as a Cancerian, I am defined with that precise and unforgettable formula: "I feel", therefore I exist. It is not about any whim of mine, it is that I am governed by the planet of cycles, tides, feelings and emotions, (at this time I trust that you have already guessed that I am referring to the romantic Moon), and I belong to the Water element, (just like my Scorpio and Pisces partners) which makes us sensitive, intuitive and inspired.

What's more: if you listen carefully to the story that Greek mythology tells about our sign, you will realize why we are so special. The Greeks say that when Hercules was performing the second of his twelve labors, a crab bit him on the big toe. Juno, who had never had the giant in her affections, was so grateful to the crab for his unexpected service that it gave him his immortality and a place in the zodiac. Excellent! Just for biting off Hercules' big toe. Don't you think?

It is true that all these characteristics seem too much for the helpless baby that I still am. What happens is that Cancerians are not very good at expressing our feelings behind this facade of security and decision, you will find yourself with a sea of doubts and feelings of insecurity; of susceptibility and hunger for affection that, if not detected in time by the people who love me and surround me, can lead me towards loneliness and depression.

But this is not an exit situation; the secret to getting out of your relationship with us Cancerians is in one-word tenderness if you give me all the love, understanding and tenderness I need to lead a happy existence, all the susceptibility and sentimentality that are always available overflow point, you will be forgotten and you will find yourself with a nice, tender and imaginative child.

I don't deny that I like to enjoy the role of voracious hoarder of affection. If I make it, I will be the happiest and most seductive child that could exist; If I can't do it, they will see me sad and withdrawn, closed in on myself, away from the world and its bustle. I'm sure that some are already calling me a term that I don't like very much, but that I will learn to accept over time: emotional black-mailer. Doesn't that sound very good? True? But there is some truth in it: when things don't go my way or when they don't give me the attention I want, I resort to tears or total withdrawal to win back their affection and protection.

My fellow sign, the Cancer girls; They are not left behind in their search for tenderness and understanding.

Only they do it in their own way: in the voices of

those around them; They want to find the universe of love and tenderness that they will always desire.

Sometimes, however, their very sensitivity leads them to find strange elements in those voices, and to seek refuge in their own world. Even more than us, Cancer girls can become perfect little machines of emotional domination, always ready to turn those around them into the servants of their sentimentality.

Due to my intuition and my ability to serve and protect others, from very early on I will be helping to care for the things and people around me. If you manage to channel these tendencies in time, I will be able to learn very quickly and contribute to the management of the home from my earliest years. I, as a typical Cancerian, can show my way of being active or passive, but you also have to look if I have characteristics of my opposite sign Capricorn, because then I can be conservative, reserved and very demanding of myself.

A very useful fact: Cancer children are prone to suffer from diseases of the digestive system and having problems with the skin, also the lungs and bronchi or a small cold will cause us annoyance; That is why it is important that they take care of us.

From Birth to One Year Cancer

Cancer children are unpredictable: for more than half an hour we can be totally consumed by crying, given over to our secret sorrows (which neither you nor I can understand), and then move on to the most harmonious and placid of states. I already know that you will make great efforts trying to understand what is happening to me and what causes these sudden moods. But don't get your hopes up about it: it is very likely that no one will be able to decipher what strange emotions lead us to go so suddenly from one state to another. In this regard, instinctive ability to register emotions that other mortals do not even suspect. That is our way of seeing and feeling the world and it is so different that it is difficult for us to understand why we are so sensitive and so changing.

But I am going to make a confession: deep down, we are incurably nostalgic people who live like this, mourning our only refuge in the mother's womb, and we do not lose the hope of one day returning to the same place where we felt safe and protected. Therefore, when If we find ourselves in one of those critical moments, the best thing they can do is keep us very close to your bodies and rock us gently. Then, we will feel that we are in the womb again and that the world is not as terrible as it seemed to us a few minutes ago.

Another method that you should not forget is to take a good bath: feeling ourselves in the water makes us remember our best moments in the womb and makes we are the happiest babies on the planet.

Because of our nostalgic spirit, it is possible that we do not develop at the same rate as babies of other signs. You will understand this more easily when you see us rejecting the solid food that you with so much patience and good intentions want us to eat, or when you see us scared and upset in the presence of strangers. Over time, however, we will adapt to the changes and gain enough confidence not to believe that every time you leave will be the last time we will see you in our lives.

From One to Two Years Cancer

Learning to walk is for us one of the most important experiences: by doing so, we discover that there is a world, full of attractive and unknown things, of whose existence we had not the slightest suspicion. But just because we dare to explore the new world that knowing how to walk gives us, does not mean that we stop facing a refuge in which we can be ourselves. Therefore, do not be surprised if in some corner of the house we set up our exclusive home, which can only be reached with our express invitation.

Our desire to keep everything will make us want to take toys to bed and sleep with them. As it will also help us become a kind of special assistant in maintaining the order of the objects in our house. Because we are so sensitive, any experience or event that threatens to jeopardize our place in the home will cause us to be in a bad mood and hinder our process of learning to speak. Therefore, do not try to force me to speak at your pace, and do not try to understand everything I say; Sometimes I don't even understand myself, and I don't really like the idea of seeing them making useless attempts to communicate with me. Simply give me time, be patient, and you will see how I can adapt to the new circumstances (even the most terrible of all: which could be the arrival of a new baby to the family).

If you want to know more I will know my, it would be interesting that they would know where I have the Moon in my Natal Map, what the sign of my Ascendant is and where the other planets are located, that way they could truly find out, like "I Feel."

Leo

From July 24 to August 23

"I WANT"

It symbolizes self-awareness and the affirmation of one's own personality. It is strength, energy and creativity. Leo presents himself to the world as a leader, to gain social recognition and conquer the place he deserves, since he is always the center of attraction and feels authoritative.

How Leo thinks

Although my companions of the other signs of the Zodiac may not like it, I am the superstar of this party: wherever I go I will always be the center of attention, the Sun around which everyone present will revolve, the leader who distributes positions and functions with the same ease with which my little Taurus friends were ecstatic following the flight of a butterfly. The fact is that my sign is ruled by Sun, the most powerful of the planets, the one that gives vital energy to our galaxy, and, as if that were not enough, I enjoy the influence of the fire element, the most active of all the elements, the one that makes the world move with its impulse and its heat. As you can see, I am a special case. As special as the story that the Greeks began to tell about me many years ago: Once upon a time there was a lion that was protected by a skin that could successfully resist the attacks of iron, bronze and stone. Hercules, the very powerful Hercules about whom so much has been said, wanted to defeat him in open combat, but he only succeeded when he strangled him with his own hands. Already victorious, Hercules covered himself with the lion's skin, and became the most unbeatable of the warriors of the time. Jupiter, to honor the feat of Hercules, gave the name of the Lion to one of the constellations that traveled through the heavens. For this reason, those born under this sign have the courage and pride of the lion and we are distinguished by a phrase that may seem pretentious to many, but which in our opinion is hardly natural: "I Want."

But I do not want them to get the impression that children of this sign are incurably conceited who want to make everyone our unconditional vassals. On the contrary, it is because of the immense capacity for affection that we possess and because of the optimism that never ceases to accompany us that we want to direct all the companies, the games and the sports in which we participate. Those who start to know me will realize that in addition to wanting to do everything my way, the Sun has endowed me with a family-sized heart that allows me to give affection and energy to everyone. It is as if he has two faces: that of the arrogant and proud child who does not allow anything to be done without his express approval, and that of the affectionate and kind baby who ends up seducing everyone. I do not like solitary games: if the luck of the Universe were in my hands, I would try to organize games in which all the children on the planet could participate, with one condition, that if, that I be the maximum leader and organizer of that game at the level planetary. If something or someone opposes this natural design of mine, I will fly into a rage and I can become intolerant and dogmatic, something like a lion wounded in its own love. But if others accept my leadership and allow me to become the center of attention of what is happening, they could enjoy the pleasure of seeing me happy and radiant, like a bright summer sun. (Do not forget that when I am still in the crib and words and words have not come to my aid, it will be my eyes and my gestures that indicate if the world has rewarded me with the attention I require).

Then you will be the only and very privileged spectators of my theatrical and dramatic displays.

Although many believe that Leo children always respond to the same characteristics, it is up to me to tell them that they are not right and that, on the contrary, even in this sign full of energy and vitality, there may be shy boys and girls and prudent, reserved in their behavior, without the exuberance that accompanies us on many occasions. Now, if for any reason I have the characteristics of my opposite sign, Aquarius, I would be an independent, creative and bright child (although devoid of the dramatic displays of the boys and girls of my sign). The same heart that makes me so sensitive and loving, so full of energy and vitality, is also the weakest part, or at least the most prone to getting sick, of my body. The back, palpitations, angina pectoris, the spinal cord can also cause me some discomfort. But don't worry: it's just the possibility, if you take care of my health, most of these problems would never happen.

From Birth to One Year Leo

We Leo babies don't like to go unnoticed: since we appear in this world we want to be the center of attention. As if we had been taking, in our mothers' wombs, an accelerated course in the art of captivating the public, we see everyone around us as potential spectators whom we must seduce with our charms.

But this desire to be the center of attention also has its good side: since we like you to always be by our side, we easily adapt to the fixed program that you present for us. With one condition: every time we require company, make sure you are there or introduce us to a visitor eager to establish communication. If neither of these two alternatives works, don't be surprised if we treat you to an endless session of crying and protesting. Don't forget: every living being is a potential playmate for us. (And a warning for those who believe that after giving us two minutes of their time, they can abandon us with impunity and continue their boring adult conversation: if they do, they will become creditors of our permanent enmity, and they will only be able to be our friends again if They prove that they really are, staying with us as long as our insatiable Leo spirit requires).

If you follow all these instructions to the letter, you

will see how gratifying it is to have a baby like us, so funny, so awake, so full of life and so willing to learn to speak in the shortest time possible.

From One to Two Years Leo

Difficult times: it could happen that we would insist on eating with one of you, and then let you know that we are not interested and that we would prefer to eat alone; or to attract the attention of those present, we would turn the cutlery, plates and food into unexpected artistic material, which would end up on the floor as proof of our undoubted artistic talent. On such occasions it is best to leave us alone in time, and prepare the space for our trips through the art world (in other words, cover the floor with newspapers, use plastic plates, cups and spoons and be ready to celebrate our genius).

Since we have such a high opinion of our dignity, do not try to take us away by force objects that may be dangerous to our physical integrity. It is better that they use their best weapons of seduction and present us with harmless toys that can gain our attention, or bring out their best comedian instincts and make us laugh. If they don't do it this way, they will have to put up with a major tantrum.

Believing ourselves to be the permanent stars of our own show makes us want to repeat, over and over again, the moment of good night. The thing is that we don't like to be alone, away from the attention of our faithful viewers.

In the end, however, fatigue will overcome us, and with the help of a half- open door that lets in a little light and the echo of other voices, we will sleep peacefully until the next day.

If you want to know more about me, it would be important for you to know where the Moon is in my Natal Map, what the sign of my Ascendant is and where the other planets are located. With this they will be able to get even closer to the wonderful world of Leo boys and girls and appreciate our "Authority".

Virgo

From August 24 to September 23

"I ANALYZE"

It symbolizes the ability to analyze, catalog, discriminate, separate, criticize, and see details and defects. They have the mission of bringing order where there is confusion and they are always ready to serve. They are proud to represent the aristocracy of work and have responsibility to get what they want.

How Virgo Thinks

As it happens to certain countries, we, Virgo children, are victims of terrible bad press. It is said that we are hypochondriacs, cold, pedantic, uninspired, fussy and reserved. We are disqualified as boring, judgmental people who, from a very early age, would be dedicated to finding the defects of the human beings who are close to us or, at least, within reach from our sight.

I am willing to accept that there is some truth in the bad press that will accompany me throughout my life, but it would be unfair to you, and to my fellow sign, if I allowed this incomplete version of my character to prosper. The truth is that I am ruled by the planet Mercury, the star of communication and the transmission of ideas, which is in charge of all the operations of thought and reason. Therefore, the key phrase of my sign, "I Analyze", is just a logical consequence of my intimate and privileged relationship with the very analytical Mercury. To confirm the privileged nature of my sign, listen to the following story: in the Iron Age, the ghost of war bloodied our planet and all the gods, one by one, decided to go to their celestial refuges. In the end, only Astrea, the pure innocent daughter of Jupiter, remained on Earth, until the barbarism became so unbearable that she also went to the heavens, and took her place in the middle of the stars, where she is known as the constellation of Virgo.

But Mercury is not alone in this story: like my Capricorn and Taurus friends, my element is Earth, which gives me a sense of order and reality that children of other signs cannot enjoy. Therefore, from a very young age I can discover the slightest flaws in the way my parents and siblings dress, the smallest disorder in the arrangement of my toys or the slightest lack of harmony in the colors that surround me. Could it be thought in parents prouder than mine, seeing the order and realism of their son? No, but do not forget, either, this decisive recommendation: because of my sharp critical spirit, because of my ability to see things that others simply cannot see, it is possible that in my early years I distance myself from other children, and end up being a lonely and withdrawn child. For this, the remedy is very easy: be understanding and close parents, always willing to talk to me, to provide me with toys and activities that allow me to keep my mind busy, and to read me stories that help me discover other worlds. Then I will be a happy and active child, creator of my own world.

As I always aspire for the best - at least intellectually and artistically - my only possible goal is the achievement of perfection. Therefore, you will see that what would easily make a child of another sign happy, in my case it is just a step towards that difficult task of making sure everything is in order as I am always dreaming of.

But that search for perfection can cause serious damage to my poor intestines, which are like the mirror in which my doubts and worries are reflected. Therefore, when I am suffering from one of my bouts of bad mood or acute self-criticism, do not try to feed me: food and worry do not go hand in hand in my sign.

My fellow girls signs share with me that love for perfection and order, that desire to analyze everything, to reduce problems to their essential elements, to know everything. However, they do not have that aggressiveness that sometimes accompanies Virgo children. Their modesty and introversion would prevent them from going to the extremes that we can sometimes go to. What we Virgo boys and girls do share is our generosity and our willingness to serve others without expecting anything in return, and without even wanting to achieve modest recognition.

Those who talk about my coldness forget that, like all other children, I am eager for affection and tenderness (perhaps even more so in my case, due to my tendency toward introversion and aloofness). If you discover this in time, you will not have to face major problems later.

And don't forget that if I have the characteristics of

my opposite sign, which is Pisces, instead of being the analytical child that you already know, I would be a dreamy, romantic and very sensitive being.

From Birth to One Year Virgo

I must admit that it is not easy to be by my side during the first three months of my existence on this planet. The slightest, most distant noise can ruin your patient efforts of several hours to get me to sleep. But do not be discouraged: your efforts will be rewarded when you witness the thoughtful and admiring way in which I discover the world, analyzing what surrounds me and foreseeing the probable dangers that lie in wait for me. (By the way, I'll tell you a secret: unlike my spectacular neighbor Leo, I don't jump into that unknown pool that is the world. My program is very different. Instead of launching myself into the conquest of admiration of everyone around me, I prefer to create the entire world in my head and, then, undertake the conquest of that universe that I already have in my imagination).

I am, I must confess, a lover of calm conversation without worries. Through it, you will be able to get everything you want from me (even making me eat in an orderly manner and according to the schedule that you have always wanted to impose on me), except when you make the mistake of letting strangers, with pretensions to be nice, want approach me and establish a supposed "conversation", which will only succeed in annoying me and ruining my peace of mind.

From One to Two Years Virgo

Unlike what happens with other children, I don't like being picked up: they will immediately see my little body wriggling, trying to find the lost freedom. On the other hand, if you read me stories and let me turn the pages and point out my favorite characters, I will be the happiest child in the world. You will see how quickly I know the name of most of the things that are around me, and how I distinguish, without the slightest doubt, the characters that appear in the stories that you will read for me.

My analytical spirit will take me to the deepest recesses of the closets of the house. There, in the midst of their forgotten treasures, I will keep my own treasures (pieces of toys, crayons, pencils, pictures). And, there is anyone who dares to intrude into the sacred space of my treasures! You will have to put up with my annoyance and legitimate anger at such an unjustified intrusion into my secret world.

Even though I don't have any problem of learning, if you try to force me to go to the bathroom at certain times, my response may be the most excruciating constipation. The reason is simple: nothing makes a Virgo child feel worse than not being able to do something his parents have tried to teach him. Therefore, by not being able to follow the rigid schedule that you try to impose on me, the humiliation and shame I feel will be reflected in my digestion.

If you want to know more about me, it would be interesting for you to know what my Ascendant is, and where I have the Moon and the other planets in my Natal Map. This way you could get even closer to the way I "Analyze" the world around me.

Libra

From September 24 to October 23

"I BALANCED"

It symbolizes the ability to relate to people to achieve the balance and complementation you need. He likes art, beauty, dialogue, as well as pleasing and harmonizing in and with the environment. He relates intellectually, sentimentally and socially with others. He has a great sense of Justice.

How Libra Thinks

As I am ruled by the planet Venus, (just like my little friend Taurus) which symbolizes love and beauty, and my element is Air - the most harmonious of all - (which I share with the children of Aquarius and Gemini) so that's why I am the most charming and attractive child ever known.The magnetism with which I am endowed makes children and adults enjoy my company and want to be by my side at all times.

It's not that I seek people's approval: it's that, by nature, I have a tendency to please others, to make them happy, to help them discover the best in them. In a word, I like to share and harmonize. Hence my key phrase is: "I Balance."

My desire to harmonize can be seen in an old story from Greek mythology. Legend has it that Teresias, a very handsome young man, managed to attract the attention of Juno. She, interested in winning the favors of the young man, let him see the mating of two snakes. Teresias asked the goddess who of the two had had more pleasure, the male or the female. Since Juno did not know, she sent the young man to Earth - once as a man and once as a woman, so that he could discover it through your own experience. When he returned, Jupiter and Juno asked him how it had gone. Teresias, who did not want to offend either of them, opted for the diploma and replied that in both conditions he had had equal pleasure. Pressured by both of them, he had to admit that as a woman he had had more pleasure. Jupiter was offended and left him blind forever. Since then, Libra (having known the feminine and masculine polarities) is the sign that has an innate sense of balance and harmony. Therefore, the symbol of Justice is a blindfolded Venus, who has a scale in one hand and a sword in the other.

If my Aries companions want to affirm their Self at all costs and bravely face all the obstacles that stand in their way, we, the boys and girls of Libra, feel stronger to the extent that more human beings are willing to share his path with us. Instead of a lone warrior, I am a team fighter, always ready to attract new playmates or business partners with my charms. (This desire to always want to share my experiences with others can cause serious problems for me: loss of self-confidence, inability to decide, tendency to ("go with the flow.") However, do not forget that if I come to possess some of the characteristics of my opposite sign Aries, I would be an impulsive, brave and determined child, who would trust my own decisions much more and who would not be so willing to share with others.

As I am an expert seducer, beings of the opposite sex will be easily attracted to my Venusians' charms, which are infallible. Such ability can sometimes turn me into the little emperor who can achieve the impossible, through the use of my magnetism. The first victims of my capacity for seduction are you, my lucky parents, who must be very attentive so as not to end up being a pair of benevolent geniuses, always ready to satisfy even my smallest desires.

Due to the influence of Venus, from a very young age I will be showing my natural inclination towards the artistic: music, painting, sculpture and everything that requires imagination and harmony, will attract me without hope.

Despite being a very healthy child, I have a predisposition to kidney disease (including diabetes). But don't worry too much: simple care and a good diet will be enough to keep my health in perfect condition.

Libra from Birth to One Year

If you see me smiling a few days after I was born, don't think that it is due to the presence of some strange gases that would be mortifying my body. No; it is a real smile, the first of many that will accompany me throughout my life as a baby and that will make you lucky and happy parents.

There will be many opportunities in which my smile will brighten the lives of those who are with me: in the bathtub, playing with water, or in the high chair, receiving the first spoonful of solid food of my life, or in the patio of the house, sharing a day with you of sun and wind.

It is not at all difficult to realize how I like to enjoy constant company: if you, or my eventual visitors and friends, are by my side, you will see me happy smiling. But if, for some reason, they leave me alone, they will have to endure my furious crying. (Of course, crying will not always be my strategy). First, I will use my most skillful methods of seduction - those that have earned me the title of "charming" - and then, I will resort to using that last resource, which is crying. Whatever my method, I recommend that you do not fall completely into the charms of my seduction; don't forget that after six months I must learn to be only.

After nine months, I will learn to enjoy the charm of

seeing myself reflected in the mirror, and I will be able to spend hours smiling at myself, amazed at being able to find myself in that place. And if you join this magical game you will make me the happiest child you have ever met.

From One to Two Years

Despite having completed my first year, I still don't like to eat alone. On the contrary, there is nothing more fun for me than that game of offered spoonful and exchanged words that my meals become. Over time, however, they will want to change roles and I will demand the transfer of the spoon to my hands. (Don't think that this change will help me improve my nutrition: on the contrary, it is quite possible that almost all of the food ends up splashing on both of our dresses, and very little actually goes into my stomach.)

Chalk, crayons, pencils become my favorite companions when I give free rein to my fabulous imagination and set out to reconstruct the world according to my very special version of harmony and aesthetics. However, my artistic tendencies are not limited to painting: at 18 months you will be able to see how I begin to follow the music with my body, and amidst laughter, I show my skill in dancing and dancing.

If you want to know more about me, I suggest you read my Natal Map and find out where my Moon is, what the sign of my Ascendant is and where the other planets are located. Then what you already know about me will become clearer and more precise, and my desire to share everything and to achieve permanent harmony in my life, it will be more understandable for you.

Scorpio

From October 24 to November 22

"I WISH"

It symbolizes the reality of a relationship, not only in the social aspect, but also in intimate emotions. It represents the desire to investigate and penetrate deeply into the human being and the hidden mysteries of nature. He interacts with the opposite sex to generate a new civilization.

How Scorpio Thinks

I must confess that I am not an easy child to understand; philosophers, psychologists, thinkers of all disciplines have dedicated entire lives to deciphering the keys to my sign. Therefore, do not declare yourself defeated when faced with the first difficulties and follow my example of my perseverance and vitality. Over time it you will realize that although it is not possible to know all my secrets, it is possible to understand the world in which I operate. To help you in your task, I give you some initial information: As like Aries, I am ruled by Mars, the planet of energy and vitality (in other words, the one that does not let us falter in any of our undertakings), and by Pluto and the planets of unexpected changes, creative forces and transformations. My element, like my friends Cancer and Pisces, is Water (only in my sign it manifests in a fixed form, which helps explain my proverbial constancy in everything I do), and in the symbol of my sign they can encounter three very different beings: the always fearsome scorpion, with its impregnable shell and its threatening stinger, the powerful and aerial eagle, and the harmless dove. If the scorpion predominates in me, it is very likely (if you do not help me in time) that I will become a stubborn and spiteful child very unwilling to forget the offenses and injustices to which he may be subjected. But if it is the eagle that takes the reins, I will be a child with protective tendencies and an overflowing and active imagination. If it were the dove that predominates in my character, I will be much more docile, spiritual, loyal, loving, willful and more peaceful.

According to Greek legend, the hunter Orion shouted that he could kill all the wild animals in the world. The gods were displeased with what Orion boasted; They sent him a monstrous scorpion, which Orion could not kill. Fatally, the scorpion stabbed him with its stinger. Zeus then placed the scorpion in the heavens in the constellation of that name and did the same with Orion, who is constantly pursued by the scorpion. Therefore, so that the scorpion does not have the letter victorious, I advise you that, from my first months, you make me the subject of a firm and calm discipline, which helps me respect the ideas and points of view of others, and allows me to forget the insults and attacks that others may direct at me. If you dedicate yourself to that task with seriousness and devotion, you will see me ascend to the highest, like the eagle or the dove, but if you take it as unimportant advice, you will have to suffer the pain of seeing me sink to the lowest.

It's not that I want to be an alarmist: I just want that from my first days you know how to interpret my silences and my tantrums, and also know how to see the danger signs in my behavior in time. It is not, however, that you should devote yourself to imposing your views on me or monitoring me relentlessly. No, the only thing I ask of you is a little attention, and intelligence, so that the immense accumulated physical energy that I possess has a positive and creative outlet. And an extra piece of advice: never argue in my presence, because even if it seems to be A poor helpless and forgetful child, I am capable of registering everything in my mind and suffering terrible nightmares that could be harmful to my mental health.

My fellow sign, Scorpio girls, have an investigative, penetrating mentality and a very good ability to intuitively grasp people's reactions. Although they appear calm and relaxed, they are more sensitive and emotional than children.

Since I belong to a fixed sign, it is possible that, over time, rheumatism attacks me.

Also don't rule out nasal colds, fractures and polyps. No. I am not very expressive when it comes to showing my feelings, but if you notice me depressed, the best thing you can do is keep me close to you and show me a lot of love and affection.

From Birth to One Year Scorpio

My arrival into this world will be marked by a cry of anguish that will scare even our poor neighbors (unless they are very far away).

And it won't be a matter of a few days: during the first months of my life on this planet, that fearsome cry of anguish will be almost a certainty if you, or some clueless visitor, dare to wake me from a peaceful and peaceful sleep. I am sure that when you see the persistence of my crying you will understand very well the signal that I am sending you: that I require you, your help, your understanding and your arms so that you can take me in your arms and I can return to my happy dreams.

From a very young age, I will demonstrate extreme sensitivity and I will surprise you with the way I am able to fix my gaze a few weeks after my birth. From these first images, I will begin to create my own world and, only later, I will launch myself headlong into conquering what surrounds me.

Any contact with a new stimulus can turned out to be a difficult experience for me. But if you act with tact and moderation, trying to understand my rhythm of adaptation to things, I will not have any major difficulties and I will come to enjoy the stimuli that previously caused me so much trouble.

From One to Two Years Scorpio

As at this age I will have already surpassed my purely contemplative state, my body and my spirit will be ready to be exercised in games that require agility and energy. Thus, you will see me running after a ball, or throwing it into the air while a scream of satisfaction comes from my throat, or receiving it in my hands, after the incredible pass that you have made to me.

As long as I am dedicated to this type of games, all my energy will be channeled in a positive way and you will not have to fear the probable mischief that my overflowing vitality may lead me to commit. (By the way, an important recommendation: due to the threat of my antics, you may have to save the best porcelain, the most valuable paintings and the most expensive electronic devices that are within my reach. This way they will avoid unnecessary conflicts and help my imagination.

I am a very loyal child to my older toys: the seduction of new toys does not suit me, and you will be wasting your time if you try to win my affection through new objects. For this reason, it is possible that for several weeks, and even months, all my interest will be concentrated in a single toy, of which I will want to exhaust all the uses and possibilities, and even take with me everywhere. This tenacity will also help me to persevere until the last moment to achieve mastery of a certain mechanism (turning on the radio, the television, the sound system, or uncovering a bottle). But I would not like to finish this paragraph without confessing that if I fail in any of my technological ventures, it is possible that the same feeling that led me to scare you and our neighbors, will reappear and my bad temper will take over me, making me launch a few kicks left and right and I didn't want to sportingly accept my momentary frustration.

If you have problems teaching me how to announce my physiological needs, I ask you not to despair, as it is very likely that this situation will be delayed for some time, and your plans to turn me into a mature and orderly being will have to be postponed for a few more days.

If you have access to my Natal Map, you will be able to find out if I acted like a Scorpio or like my opposite sign, Taurus, in which case I would be a very calm, patient and silent child, as well as capricious and possessive.

In order for them to reach my deepest secrets, they have to investigate where I have the Moon, what the sign of my Ascendant is and where the other planets are located. Only then could you know what I am and how much I "Desire" to be constantly transforming and renewing myself.

Sagittarius

From November 23 to December 21

"I SEE"

It symbolizes abstract thinking and the higher mind. It is the beginning of relationships with the outside world, adventure and leaving your environment to see and know what is beyond. It represents philosophy, culture, religion, faith and the vision of truth, which it defends to the end.

How Sagittarius Thinks

If you notice me restless in the crib, if you see my desire to leave the place you have designated me, if you discover an inexplicable shine in my eyes (as if instead of seeing you I were discovering wonderful worlds of adventure and play), it is not that something strange is happening to me: it is that I am showing what it does to us , the children of Sagittarius, so different from the friends of the other signs of the Zodiac: our love for Freedom, our desire to turn everything - even the most serious things - into a reason for play, due to our desire to know the whole Universe.

These tendencies have an explanation that almost completely convinces me: on the one hand, like Pisces, I am ruled by the planet Jupiter, the planet of benevolence and understanding, the most jovial of the stars, the one with the permanent smile and the hand always ready to help those who need it; and on the other side, like Aries and Leo, I belong to the element of Fire, the most restless and mobile of the elements. What's more: if you look at the symbol of my sign, you will realize that it is a centaur, that mythological figure that is half man and half horse. Legend has it that Apollo and Diana were the instructors who taught the centaur Chiron, who was famous for his hunter qualities, medicine, art and prophecy. Chiron was considered the wisest and fairest of all the centaurs; upon his death Zeus Jupiter gave him the honor of a place in the heavens in the constellation of Sagittarius. Now you will understand why, in our small being, the agility and physical strength of the animal, and the intelligence and logical capacity of humans, come together.

That's why, at the least expected moment, you will see me crawling on my way to freedom and the outdoors, or trying to discover the most intricate secrets of the world in which I live. When I get the opportunity to speak, you will have to be careful not to lose your patience in the face of the overwhelming number of questions with which I will constantly bombard you. But even so, due to my playful and benevolent nature, what in other children might sound like a merciless and merciless attack on their suffering parents, in me is accepted as another grace of my personality, uncomplicated and curious.

Since I am so nice and so playful, being rejected by someone can become a real tragedy: then, you will see abundant tears in my eyes and only your understanding and tenderness will help me return to my normal state.

Our sisters, Sagittarius girls, are so similar to us that many would be tempted to doubt their femininity. When you see them always at our side, sharing the same games, running the same dangers, and making the same physical efforts, the less understanding will try to remind them of their feminine nature and the need for them to behave like "real ladies." But it won't help much: Sagittarius girls are as given to outdoor games and love of freedom as we are.

When the time comes to teach me the rules necessary to live in society, please do not try to impose them by force, making use of law in spaces open to arbitrariness and coercion, because that will only awaken the rebel. What's in me? On the other hand, if you try to reason with me, showing me the logic behind the rules you are trying to teach me, rest assured that I will learn very quickly and without any problem. What's more: if you are as sensitive as all parents of Sagittarius children should be, living this learning process with me is going to be a fascinating and happy experience. So fascinating, that you could end up being my best accomplices and playmates.

So much energy and activity brings with it certain risks: a trip, a fall, a collision with a half- open door, an unexpected dive into a pool, are possibilities that cannot be forgotten when it comes to a Sagittarius boy or girl. As for diseases, the most common are respiratory and nervous diseases.

From Birth to One Year Sagittarius

As if it were an energetic announcement of the very agile days to come, my entry into this world will be characterized by a constant kicking that can only calm the deepest of my dreams. Soon, my initial kicking will have gained in sophistication and my constant and varied movements will be the best source of inspiration for athletes who have the privilege of observing me.

After six months, my extraordinary vocation athleticism could become a nightmare for the poor people in charge of changing my diapers: untimely jumps, furious kicks, quick 180 degree turns, could end the patience of the most understanding of humans. However, such a unique athletic activity will turn you, my lucky parents, into beings of enviable agility, possessors of a physical condition that only athletes at the highest competitive level can aspire to.

Don't believe, however, that my muscular and recreational activity is reduced to the heroic moment of changing diapers. On the contrary; Almost every moment of my life as a baby is marked by my constant movement and my desire to explore everything that is beyond my sight. That's why, when the time comes to crawl, the old borders of my world collapse, and with the help of my body, which has become a tireless motor, I set out to conquer the unknown. If by this date you already know me well enough, I am sure that you will not try to keep me reduced to the narrow space of my corral or my crib. Trying to do so would be the worst of mistakes, because instead of having the privilege of my usual smile and natural optimism, they would have to face my cries of indignation and protest.

I love everything new: the first dip in the bathtub, the enjoyment of my first solid foods, my initial forays into the fascinating outside world. (The latter, above all, fills me with unmatched happiness and allows me to get in touch with what I like most in outdoor life).

From one to two years Sagittarius

The great actor in me will set out to conquer the world even before he turns one year old.

Every adult meeting will become an opportunity to show my great histrionic skills: I will jump, I will sing, I will speak long incomprehensible tirades, I will transform my face into a variety of very funny faces, and everyone will be admired by my theatricality and ease.

However, not all of mine is pure physical action and theatrical games. I also like to cultivate my spirit through reading (in which you will be a great help) comic books and adventures. Since at this age I will already be speaking in a row, it is very likely that you will have to listen to my very varied stories about animals and children (in which, almost always, I am the protagonist who is in charge of protecting kittens, dogs and all kinds of animals). My desire to know everything, and to take over the outside world at great speed, could cause you some headaches. You, for example, may worry about my tendency to strike up conversations with strangers, and to look at almost everyone as a potential friend. See, however, the positive aspect of this tendency: when you have to go with me to a dinner or to some invitation that is given to you, instead of the withdrawn and shy child. You will have a little public relations expert, who will feel very happy and calm anywhere, and will play until tired and fall asleep wherever you are.

If you knew my Natal Map, you could know how many characteristics I possess from my opposite sign, Gemini (then you will find out about my unmatched communication possibilities and my extreme versatility). The same thing could happen with my Ascendant and with the position of the Moon and the other planets. Then, you would have a more precise idea of my personality and the way in which I "Understand" my peers.

Capricorn

From December 22 to January 20

"I USE"

It symbolizes respect, organization, order and authority. You need stability to acquire power and social position. Having learned and assimilated all the stages of the previous signs, you know what you want, what you should do, and how to use experiences to get what you want.

How Capricorn Thinks

From one sign to another, everything can change very quickly: if my Sagittarius friends they were uncomplicated, forgetful and optimistic, We, Capricorn children, come into this world full of seriousness, perseverance and ambition. It is not our whim, it is that we are in the kingdom of Saturn, the planet of discipline and responsibility, and we were lucky to have the Earth element, which ensures stability and practicality. For this reason, in the mythology of the Greeks and Romans, our sign is personified in the god Pan. Legend has it that during the war between the gods of Olympus and the Titans of the Earth, the former were thrown into Egypt. But they were pursued by Typhon, the leader of the giants. To escape danger, each of the gods had to change their physiognomy. Pan jumped into the Nile, and transformed the upper part of his body into a goat and the lower part into a fish. Guided by the invisible hands of Jupiter into a deadly trap, the Titans fell victim to the lightning and thunder of the God of gods. Then Pan was rewarded by Jupiter, who gave him a place in the sky, where today he is known as Capricorn, for his originality in transforming into a goat-fish.

Perhaps due to these circumstances, my image does not correspond to what you may have of a child my age.

But don't be discouraged: instead of finding in me the typical traits that every little child should exhibit, you will be able to enjoy my maturity, my common sense and my tenacity to achieve; at all costs, the objectives that I set for myself, even if I have to spend several days achieving them. For example, when you dare to deny me a wish, my response will not be tearful or spectacular. In silence, I will wait until the opportunity arrives to restate my point of view. With infinite patience, I will use every little opportunity that comes my way to get closer to my goal. In the end, when you give in to my silent demands, you will not even realize that everything has been the result of my silent and patient work.

Our travel companions, Capricorn girls, show from very early on a definite inclination for home life. From their first games, they will love to put themselves in the role of mothers (to the point of suggesting the reversal of roles with their real mothers: "You are the baby and I am the mommy", you will hear them say when they have the opportunity to speak).

But if perseverance can help me in my studies and in my life in general, Ambition, on the other hand, can lead me down the terrible path of opportunism. Therefore, you must be very careful to distinguish between my very edifying tendency to achieve what I set out to do, and my inclination to use people to achieve my goals. Forgetting the latter can help me become a little manipulator, who would be willing to use those closest to me to achieve his purposes. Although I am in very good health, rashes can appear on my very sensitive skin, and in moments of nervousness and tension, my stomach can be affected. They should be equally careful with my knees, which despite being transported everywhere, can suffer some damage due to the continuous use I make of them.

From Birth to One Year Capricorn

I imagine you have already realized how difficult it is to get a smile from me. You will have tried your best tricks, you will have consulted experts, you will have used your most effective tricks, but you will have achieved nothing. But from this obvious fact, do not jump to false conclusions: it is not that I am sick, or that I do not like their pampering and their graces, or that I was born with a natural and inexplicable distaste for other human beings.The only true explanation for my constant frown can only be found in the simple and blunt fact that I am a very serious baby.

I said serious, not sad or bitter. Serious means that I take life in a very mature way since I came into this world. No unjustified smiles or permanent laughter. Therefore, when my face produces a smile it is because I have learned something new and I am now capable of practicing it.

Now it's easier to understand why I frown: it's nothing more than the way I show my deep state of concentration when I'm trying to learn something new; and since I am persistent and do not give up at the first difficulty that comes my way, you will be able to see me for hours entire, frowning brow, attentive and fixed gaze, trying to learn the key to some mechanism or movement.

From One to Two Years Capricorn

When I am already taking my first steps and can walk around the entire house on my own, my organizational desire will increase and all the furniture, corners and objects that I find in my path will become material for my increased interest in order and order and curiosity. However, it is good to remind you that my organizational desire is accompanied by an unusual sense of self-criticism, which leads me to correct myself, with unusual severity: "That is not done, never do it again," you will hear me say to myself after having turned an entire closet drawer upside down, or scattering all the papers on the desk on the floor. It is hardly obvious that with a child as disciplined and conscientious as me, you will not have to be as severe as you will have to be with children of other characteristics. We ourselves will be the first to realize the mistake made and we will try to correct it immediately. What's more, given our love for discipline and hard work, you will be able to guide us towards practical and useful tasks from a very early age (such as taking the clothes out of the dryer, helping to organize our toys or tidying up the house).

If you find out, through my Map Natal, I have the characteristics of the opposite sign, Cancer, you will see that I am a dreamer, sensitive and imaginative. Likewise, it would be important for you to know where my Moon is, what the sign of my Ascendant is, and where the other planets are located. Then, you could have a more accurate picture of my vocation as an organizer and other qualities of why "I Use."

Aquarius

From January 21 to February 19

"I KNOW"

It symbolizes the unity of spirit, mind and matter. It is elevated, intuitive, investigative and innovative thinking; the advance that makes possible advances and discoveries at a technological level and new humanitarian values. It is also the sign of friendship, altruism and universal love.

How Aquarius Thinks

Having been born under the influence of Saturn and Uranus, the planets of responsibility and originality respectively, and because Air is my element, I, like all Aquarius children, come into the world with an overwhelming passion for everything investigate and experiment. As if we were little machines designed to find the truth and to invent the least common things, our entire being will be dedicated, from a very early age, to investigating the keys to what surrounds us and to looking for new and unknown uses for the most mortal things. Hence the key phrase that identifies is "I Know."

In Greek mythology it is said that Deucalion reigned over a race that was in total decline. Jupiter destroyed it with a flood, but not before telling Deucalion to build a chest and lock himself inside with his wife, Pyrrha. When the flood ended, the chest was at the top of Mount Parnassus. From there, Deucalion and his wife headed to Delphi to ask the Oraclehow they could repopulate the human race. Jupiter, I ordered them to throw stones back. The stones that Pyrrha threw b ecame women, and the ones her husband threw became they transformed into men. Thus, the land was repopulated. Therefore, Aquarius is the sign of renewal and recreation of an entire community.

My inventor soul is complemented by my Oceanic love for humanity. Therefore, from a very young age you will see me trying to change whatever is within my power in order to make the lives of my parents, siblings and friends easier and more fun. Many times, however, this immense love for humanity is not manifested openly, and some may come to think that I am a distant and cold child, not given to sharing with my peers. From now on I tell you that you couldn't be more wrong. In fact, I am so interested in building a better future for all my fellow human beings that sometimes I forget about the flesh and blood beings around me.

Due to the contradictory influence of Saturn and Uranus, I keep fluctuating between two opposite poles: that of originality (which allows me to be a creator without borders), and that of responsibility (which makes me remain tied to what is normal and established). If Saturn prevailed completely, the revolutionary and creative breath of Aquarius would disappear, and he would end up being a conservative child, without any impulse for change and renewal. But if the opposite were to happen, and everything was left in the hands of Uranus, the desire for universal transformation and change, I could become an ardent anarchist, unwilling to understand that not all change can be total and that some of the things of the old order must be preserved; The ideal would be to achieve a balance between these two tendencies: then, the ideal of renewal would be linked to the realism of those who know that not everything can be changed at once. Sometimes, when one of the two tendencies radically prevails, my natural creativity can be wasted, and I could reach the end of adolescence without having been able to develop any of my talents.

Being creative and innovative makes me a child that is not very easy to handle. Always on the move, I put my parents in trouble by trying to keep up with my crazy pace and understand my many investigative adventures. However, my charming way of being and my creative and adventurous spirit are enough reward for the discomfort and physical fatigue that my behavior can generate in you.

My travel companions, the Aquarian girls, would enjoy seeing themselves as first dancers in one of the best companies in the world, or leaders of a country. Not because they are power-hungry girls, but because they always aspire to be in positions from where they can most effectively help humanity.

Those who have read this far will have already suspected what my problems may be: If you have thought that due to my excessive idealism I can fall into useless and fruitless suffocation, you are very close to the truth, and if you have believed that my desire to renewal can turn me into a stubborn and inflexible creature, prisoner of a cause or an idea, they will have been right twice. Hence, an education aimed at making me see the need for harmony and balance in my companies and creations is fundamental.

And don't forget to take very close care of me blood system. Since I am an Air sign, circulatory functions are the most important in my body and also the most prone to deteriorate. Via Uranus, I am predisposed to ankle sprains, cramps and fractures of all kinds.

From Birth to One Year Aquarius

Unpredictable: that's how Aquarius babies are. Since the remote times when we were in mom's womb, we always had a contrary schedule:

When mom wanted to go to rest, we would do our nighttime exercises, or practice our favorite musical instrument. Therefore, even our entry into this world can be unpredictable and irregular.

Once here, things don't change much for us: all attempts to impose a fixed eating schedule on me fail in the face of our constant mood swings. Thus we can spend long hours without wanting to try anything that is offered to us and, suddenly, feel a devouring hunger and ask very insistently for what we had been offered, without any response from us, for a long time. Don't believe, however, that all this is intentional and that Aquarius babies are little experts in the art of torture. No: it is just a difficult period in our development that, when overcome, it will give enough space for you to begin teaching me the rules and schedules I need to lead a normal life.

Because everything about us is so unpredictable, we are likely to crawl at four months, stand at six, and walk at six and let us walk to the ten, as is also the fact that we continue crawling until fourteen months.

From One to Two Years Aquarius

Our rigorous individualism becomes more radical as we move beyond our first year. In all cases, even the smallest, we demonstrate our radical independence and our desire to do things our own way. For us, for example, the meal time can become a real tragedy, if we feel that you want to force a certain dish on us. It is not that we do not value your culinary efforts and your love for us, it is that we want to do everything at our own pace, without external pressures. And don't forget that when we tip over our plate, or stand on the chair, we are simply saying that we are already satisfied and that any other effort to make us eat will have no effect.

Our independent and investigative spirit can lead us to dangerous situations (such as playing with electrical outlets and installations). In these cases, you must remove us from the site and show us the dangers posed by handling these types of facilities. Of course: don't forget to give us an alternative toy. Otherwise we will feel unfairly punished.

As a good researcher that I am, I ask my parents to investigate my Natal Map, to know if I have the characteristics of my opposite sign, Leo. Case in which he would be a generous, optimistic and magnanimous child, endowed with great creative capacity. If, on the same Natal Map, you observe where the Moon is, what is the sign of my Ascendant and where the other planets are located, you will be able to penetrate even further into the secrets of our personality and learn more about what I am like and what I am that "I Know."

Pisces

From February 20 to March 20

"I BELIEVE"

It symbolizes kindness, beneficence and helping others, even at the cost of self-denial and personal sacrifice or suffering. He is tolerant, emotional, sensitive, kind, philanthropic and humanitarian. In general, he has a deep spiritual faith and a great inventive and imagination.

How Pisces Thinks

A the outset, I'm going to tell you a story: Have you ever noticed the symbol of my sign? If they have, they will have seen two fish looking in opposite directions. Well, the Greeks - who had an imagination almost as rich as that of the Pisceans - invented the following story: one day Aphrodite and Eros (the goddess and child-god of Love) were on the banks of the Euphrates River when Typhoon, a monster with the property of breathing fire, surprised them. To escape from the monster, the two jumped into the waters of the river, where they transformed into two inseparable fish, which then ascended to the heavens to become the constellation of Pisces and symbolize, forever, Love and Companionship.

You may wonder: And if they became such good companions, why do they appear looking in opposite directions? The answer is simple and complex at the same time: just as the characters in the fable that I told you in the previous paragraph were two, the planets that govern my destiny are also two, Jupiter and Neptune, and although the two can walk together, sometimes (as Aphrodite and Eros did in the story), most of the time they represent different and even opposite things. Jupiter, I must decide, is the planet of benevolence and goodness, that of selfless help to others, that of universal solidarity. Neptune, for its part, is the planet of dreams, fantasy and illusions, the one that encourages escape to other worlds, the one that brings the hidden and the unknown to everyday life.

Now think about what a child can be like governed by those two profound influences. Do it and you will meet this sensitive and benevolent being, who enjoys taking on his shoulders the sufferings and sorrows of all of humanity, who makes his neighbor's pain his own, who suffers firsthand what is happening somewhere far away, who is always willing to take the place of others when it comes to assuming pain and adversity, who has a unique intuition (that's why, if from a very young age I manage to see things that you can't even imagine, don't be scared: it's just an effect of my predisposition to discover the hidden), who can create entire worlds of fantasy and dream (where he will feel protected from the horrors and difficulties of the everyday world), and whose key phrase is an immense "I Believe ", which summarizes all the traits that make the Pisces child such a special being.

As you can see, I am not an easy character at all. If you want to be my friends and help me in the difficult task of facing the world, I suggest that you try to be understanding, that you do not get angry with my continuous escapes into fantasy worlds and that, above all, do not try to impose their points of view on me, nor restrict my sensitivity. This does not mean, however, that it does not require serious and constant discipline. On the contrary, if you do not try to teach me some minimum standards, I could end up being a capricious and crying child, very prone to taking refuge in his dream world and with the dangerous tendency to fall into the networks of self- pity. Ultimately, I cannot give you a definitive remedy but I can, at least, give you a not-very-secret key: use tenderness and softness (without forgetting, of course, discipline), get close to my heart first and then yes, try to shape my mind and my will, and do not be afraid to fall, from time to time, into my world of intuition and fantasy: over time you will realize that it is worth it and that pure and simple realism is boring and heavy.

My companions, Pisces girls, have marked artistic inclinations and dream of being (although on many occasions they can be) film or theater actresses, great dancers or hardworking composers and performers. If, from a very young age, my classmates want to turn the living room of the house, or their own crib, into a stage to show their artistic abilities, take it as something perfectly natural: a frustration at such a young age could become a major denial over time.

As we want to carry on our shoulders the burden of

the destiny of all Humanity, our poor feet are the first candidates to suffer various types of diseases and accidents. On the other hand, my element is Water, but in a mutable form, which gives me an exaggerated sensitivity that could lead me to suffer various nervous and emotional disorders.

From Birth to One Year Pisces

Coming to this world is not easy for me: after having been living in the placid, aquatic and happy world of the mother's womb, and now having to face the coldness, rigidity and light of this new space, it is something that only it can be done with a heartbreaking scream, which is what we do in most cases. A dim light in the room and a quick hug from my mother could help my first contacts with this world not be so traumatic.

But things don't end there: my nervous and emotional character will continue to express itself throughout these first months of life. It will be up to you to be understanding and tender enough to understand that my crying is not a trick of a spoiled baby, but a trait of my psychological behavior, and that my constant search for the mother's breast or a bottle does not obey my insatiable appetite alone, but also a need to find a refuge for my tensions and insecurities

Not everything about me, however, is so gloomy or worrying: you will have the opportunity to discover my extraordinary acting skills and my acute ability to imitate the voices and gestures of those around me. What's more, my skills reach the very field of music, because after six months I start trying my first solos and, if you accompany me, you could be witnesses and protagonists of my first duets.

From One to Two Years Pisces

Learning to walk is not our forte: at first, the fear of the unknown will take over me and can go to the point of crawling again (Here between us, I tell you that one of my strongest fears is mechanical objects. (they make a lot of noise. That's why vacuum cleaners and other electrical appliances are not to my liking).

When I have to share with other babies my age, I will need your help and encouragement, because my nervous nature and my tensions can make me feel insecure when it comes to playing with my contemporaries.

Thanks to my theatrical skills, it is very **i**t is likely that on certain occasions I will try to manipulate them with one of my stage routines. It will be up to you to decide correctly if it is a trick of mine or if, in reality, something is affecting me. I know that it is not an easy task, because sometimes one thing is almost indistinguishable from the other: for example, it is not easy to know if my crying in the bathtub is because I do not want to leave the refuge of the water, or if something really bothers me is hurting or bothering. Baby warning to parents: become good psychologists.

Since I'm so affectionate, don't be surprised if I ask you to sleep with me until I fall asleep. For me it is a way to show them my affection and to have them close when I want to rest and sing the lyrics of the new song I learned that day.

A reading of my Natal Map could allow you to know how many characteristics I possess from my opposite sign, Virgo. If this happens, he would be an analytical, studious and discriminating child, governed by the firm principle of achieving perfection in everything he does. Through the same Natal Map, you could find out where I have the Moon, what the sign of my Ascendant is, and where the other planets are located. With all that information, you could undertake the task of deciphering my imagination and how "I Believe" with greater chances of success.

The date of Birth in Astrology

On the date, time and place in which the child was born, there were 10 planets in the sky located in specific positions with respect to the different zodiacal constellations. These planets have a very important effect on the lives of each of us. And it depends on our knowledge that we can fully develop all the energies that these planets offer us.

It is almost impossible to find a natal chart or astrological chart that is good or bad (rather easy or difficult) in and of itself. It all depends on each person's personality, how they accept and learn to develop cosmic energies and to what extent they manage to know themselves. Astrology is just a guide that shows a person how to develop and discover the potential they have in their being. When a person realizes the potential they have, they will be able to face this world of constant changes in which we live much better equipped.

It is very important to have knowledge of where the planets were at the time of birth; to be able to do a complete study and interpretation of your child's birth map, because this is the stage in which he depends and needs his parents the most to be understood and well guided in life. I recommend that you have the experience of getting to know the child you love so much better, through this ancient science that is Astrology.

For this you need an astrological interpretation that will give you the answers to your questions, based on the exact data of the birth.

Later, you will be able to appreciate that none of us belongs to a single zodiac sign: we are a combination of several signs, which, of course, makes us more interesting and complex than we think, we imagine ourselves.

Thank you Mom for Understanding me!

WRITE TO THE AUTHOR

The Author would like to thank you in advance for writing to tell him a little about what you liked and how you benefited from this book.

The Author continues to do his research on Astrological studies of children. That is why we imagine that many readers will have comments, criticisms or questions to ask.

To write to the Author, or ask him your questions, you can do so by addressing your e-mail to:

MARIO CESAR
mariocesar2711@gmail.com

Biography

Undertaking his legendary search for truth and from a very early age, Mario Cesar, renowned Argentine astrologer, has been interested in the studies of Astrology the ancient science of the cosmos and the stars.

In the beginning he studied astrological disciplines in Argentina and Brazil, also participating in conferences, congresses and disciplinary activities in spiritualist centers and advanced studies in mystical experiences in the Amazon jungle.

After his time in the South ended with great achievements and influenced by the stars, he decided to continue and begin a new era in North America, New York, where he has continued his permanent practice.

Today, in New York, he writes daily and weekly horoscopes for the main media outlets in the city and also in other states. He is also interviewed by different radio and television stations. He was the producer of his own television program, in which He answered questions from the public live and direct. He also has his own consultancy.

To achieve the interpretation of a birth chart, Mario Cesar relies on Astrology. Its main innovation has been to find the relationship between the psychic, the physical and the emotional well-being of each person, aware of the influence of the stars in their daily lives.

www.ingramcontent.com/pod-product-compliance
Lightning Source LLC
LaVergne TN
LVHW050557160826
845677LV00011B/2345

* 9 7 9 8 8 9 5 6 9 5 4 1 8 *